CONCERNING THE ANGELS

SOBRE LOS ÁNGELES

CONCERNING THE ANGELS

SOBRE LOS ÁNGELES

POEMS

RAFAEL ALBERTI

TRANSLATED FROM THE SPANISH
BY JOHN MURILLO

FOUR WAY BOOKS
TRIBECA

LIBRARY OF CONGRESS CATALOGING-IN-PUBLICATION DATA

Names: Alberti, Rafael, 1902-1999, author. | Murillo, John, translator. |
  Alberti, Rafael, 1902-1999. Sobre los ángeles. | Alberti, Rafael,
  1902-1999. Sobre los ángeles. English.
Title: Concerning the angels = (Sobre los ángeles) / poems by Rafael
  Alberti ; translated from the Spanish by John Murillo.
Other titles: Sobre los ángeles
Description: New York : Four Way Books, 2025. | Parallel text in Spanish
  and English.
Identifiers: LCCN 2024038843 (print) | LCCN 2024038844 (ebook) | ISBN
  9781961897427 (trade paperback) | ISBN 9781961897434 (ebook)
Subjects: LCSH: Alberti, Rafael, 1902-1999--Translations into English. |
  LCGFT: Poetry.
Classification: LCC PQ6601.L2 S613 2025 (print) | LCC PQ6601.L2 (ebook) |
  DDC 861/.62--dc23/eng/20240826
LC record available at https://lccn.loc.gov/2024038843
LC ebook record available at https://lccn.loc.gov/2024038844

This book is manufactured in the United States of America and printed on acid-free paper.

Four Way Books is a not-for-profit literary press. We are grateful for the assistance we receive from individual donors, public arts agencies, and private foundations including the NEA, NEA Cares, Literary Arts Emergency Fund, and the New York State Council on the Arts, a state agency.

We are a proud member of the Community of Literary Magazines and Presses.

INDICE | CONTENTS

Acknowledgments

INTRODUCTION

Begun just five years after T.S. Eliot published *The Waste Land*, and completed the year before Federico García Lorca was to start on what would eventually become *Poet in New York*, Rafael Alberti's *Sobre los ángeles* is a monument—albeit a severely neglected monument—of early twentieth-century literature. Like Eliot, who sought to capture something of the despair of post-war London, and Lorca, who, while traveling through parts of North America and the Caribbean, bore witness to the consequences of industry, both its worship and eventual collapse, Alberti penned a masterwork of social and psychic malaise as deserving as any of its place in the global canon. A masterwork which, though all but forgotten by English language readers of poetry, we might find especially relevant today given its treatment of themes and realities one fears recurring, if not chronic.

By the time Alberti published this collection, he was already a poet of stature in his native Spain. Born Rafael Alberti Merello, December 16, 1902, in the Puerto de Santa María region of Cádiz, he was, along with Lorca, Luis Buñuel, Salvador Dalí and several other notables, a member of a loose collective of artists and intellectuals that has come to be known as "The Generation of '27." (The name alludes to the date of their first official meeting, held on the tercentenary of the death of the poet Luis de Góngora. But as C.B. Morris points out in his brilliant study, *A Generation of Spanish Poets, 1920-1936*, it "magni[fies] the significance" of their connection to Góngora, and serves only as a shorthand reference for a group of friends of roughly the same age "who were never fused by a programme into a clearly defined school.") His first collection, *Marinero en Tierra* (1925), was selected for the National Literature Prize by a panel of judges that included novelist Gabriel Miró and poet Antonio Machado. He followed with other collections such as *La Amante* (1926) and *Cal y Canto* (1929), each widely acclaimed in its own right. With such early success, one imagines this might have been a time of great joy for the young Alberti.

But as productive as these years were for the poet, they found his country at a crossroads. Spain, though neutral in the First World War, was nonetheless adversely affected and left, years later, still reeling in its aftermath. A suffering economy. Strained infrastructure. Labor strikes and food riots. A long-lasting chasm between countrymen whose loyalties were split between the Allied forces on the one side and the Central powers on the other. Such instability made possible the juntas that would shape Spain for what must have felt then like the foreseeable future. By the time Alberti hit his stride as a poet, Spain was under the dictatorial rule of one Captain General Miguel Primo de Rivera, father of José Antonio Primo de Rivera, who, in turn, would one day father the fascist Falange Española. The country Alberti knew and loved as a child had become a foreign and hostile land. Though he claims not to have known much about politics at the time, and would only come to understand much later such words as "Republic, Fascism, liberty," he could definitely feel the landscape changing. "I had lost a paradise," Alberti writes in his memoir, *The Lost Grove*, "the Eden of those early years: my happy, bright and carefree youth."

This was also a period of great personal suffering for the poet. In addition to the world's woes and his own declining health, other sources of discontent included "[a]n impossible love that had been bruised and betrayed during moments of confident surrender; the most rabid feelings of jealousy which would not let me sleep and caused me to coldly contemplate a calculated crime during the long sleepless nights; the sad shadow of a friend who had committed suicide. . . . Unconfessed envy and hate. . . . [E]mpty pockets that could not even warm my hands. . . . My family[,] silent or indifferent in the presence of this terrible struggle that was reflected on my face and in my very being . . . [M]y displeasure with my earlier work . . . all this and more.

"What," Alberti asks, "was I to do? How was I to speak or shout or give form to that web of emotions in which I was caught? How could I stand up straight once again and extricate myself from those catastrophic depths into which I had sunk[?]" The only solution for Alberti, as for any poet, was to write his way through. Initially, without any consideration of form or convention, almost automatically, and in feverish fits. Some nights, he would rise from bed to scrawl, in the dark, lines he could barely decipher come morning. Within the span of two years, Alberti would not only have given vent to his sorrows, he would also have written what many consider his magnum opus.

Sobre los ángeles was published in early 1929 to mixed critical reception. For the most part, critics praised Alberti's new direction. One such critic was José Martínez Ruiz, for whom the collection "signal[ed] [Alberti's] having reached 'the highest peak of lyric poetry.'" Still, there were one or two others, like poet Juan Ramón Jiménez, a personal hero and early champion of Alberti, who disparaged the latter's "disjointed prattling," finding it too radical a departure from his previous work. (Both Morris and Alberti, it may be interesting to note, surmise that Jiménez's critique had less to do with the book itself and more to do with a personal qualm, with his having felt abandoned by a generation of younger poets who had previously considered him a guiding force but were now blazing their own trails.) In toto, however, the years have been kind to Alberti, with the vast majority of critics and scholars in the field (albeit outside the continental United States) recognizing the collection's merit.

While it is true that these poems mark a stylistic, thematic, and tonal shift, Alberti's rigor, his attention to detail, remain constant. His choices, deliberate. When discussing, for instance, some of the structural considerations in the manuscript, Alberti remarked that "the short, controlled and concentrated verse line I had been writing gradually became longer and more in keeping with the movement of my imagination in those days." If these were poems drafted in the dark, they were also poems thought through, worked for, and revised in the full light of day. As concerns the cryptic images, the often opaque associations, in many of the poems—which were some of the key annoyances among Alberti's detractors—we would do well to remember our Lorca who, in an unrelated essay, reminds us that there exist poems "that respond to a purely poetic logic and follow the constructs of emotion and poetic architecture;" our Lorca who, many scholars, such as his biographer Ian Gibson, believe, carried with him on his voyage across the Atlantic a copy of *Sobre los ángeles*.

Speaking of Lorca, it's worth mentioning at this point that until his assassination in August of 1936, he and Alberti were often mentioned in tandem, as the two shining lights of "The Silver Age" of Spanish poetry. Friends and rivals, they shared not only a common appreciation of Andalusian folk art, respect for classical verse forms, and, paradoxically, a penchant for innovation, but nearly parallel literary careers—each publishing roughly the same number of books within the same timespan to, more or less, the same acclaim. By many accounts, Alberti was even considered the superior poet, the more versatile technician, equal to Lorca in imagination. Whereas Lorca died young, Alberti would live to age 96, write well over thirty books of verse and prose, and become, like Lorca, one of Spain's most celebrated poets. His honors include, in addition to the 1924-1925 National Prize for Literature, the International Lenin Peace Prize, the prestigious Premio Cervantes, and the America Award for lifetime achievement, whose other honorees include Aimé Césaire, José Saramago, Eudora Welty, and Mario Vargas Llosa. And yet, while any decent bookstore in the U.S. will carry a variety of Lorca translations—*In Search of Duende*, *Poet in New York*, his selected and collected poems, his plays—Alberti has fallen into relative obscurity.

In 2022, the University of California Press reissued Ben Belitt's selected Alberti as part of their "Voices Revived" series. Prior to this, Belitt's collection, originally published in 1966, had been unavailable for years. Or, rather, available only through second-hand booksellers and websites. The same is true of Mark Strand's 1982 selection of translated Alberti titled *The Owl's Insomnia*. In 2001, City Lights published Christopher Sawyer-Lauçanno's translation of *Sobre los ángeles* but that too has gone out of print. While it is beyond the scope of this introduction to speculate upon the reasons behind this diminished interest, perhaps it is not too much to lament it, to recognize it as a tremendous loss for us all.

This volume is in no way intended to serve as *The Definitive Alberti*, but rather as a humble attempt to share with a new generation of readers an important, maybe indispensable, voice.

JOHN MURILLO

BROOKLYN, MARCH 2024

WORKS CITED

Alberti, Rafael. *Sobre los ángeles.* Editorial Losada, Buenos Aires: 1952; Alianza Editorial, Madrid: 1982.

Alberti, Rafael. *The Lost Grove,* translated and edited by Gabriel Berns. University of California Press, Berkeley: 1976.

Alberti, Rafael. *Selected Poems,* edited by Ben Belitt. University of California Press, Berkeley: 1966.

Morris, C.B. *A Generation of Spanish Poets, 1920-1936.* Cambridge University Press, London: 1969.

Oh, Brian. "Lorca in New York." The Seventh Wave: September 30, 2016. www.theseventhwave.org/brian-oh/.

ENTRANCE

ENTRADA

PARAÍSO PERDIDO

A través de los siglos
por la nada del mundo,
yo, sin sueño, buscándote.

Tras de mí, imperceptible,
sin rozarme los hombros,
mi ángel muerto, vigía.

¿Adónde el Paraíso,
sombra, tú que has estado?
Pregunta con silencio.

Ciudades sin respuesta,
ríos sin habla, cumbres
sin ecos, mares mudos.

Nadie lo sabe. Hombres
fijos, de pie, a la orilla
parada de las tumbas,

me ignoran. Aves tristes,
cantos petrificados,
en éxtasis el rumbo,

ciegas. No saben nada.
Sin sol, vientos antiguos,
inertes, en las leguas

PARADISE LOST

Throughout the centuries,
through the nothingness of the world,
I, without sleep, search for you.

Behind me, imperceptible,
without touching my shoulders,
my dead angel keeps watch.

Where is Paradise,
Shadow, you who have been there?
A silent ask.

Cities of no answers,
rivers of no speech, summits
of no echoes, silent seas.

Nobody knows. Men,
stone-still, standing on the edge
of graves,

ignore me. Sad birds,
their petrified cantos,
in ecstatic formation, fly

blind. They know nothing.
Without sun, ancient winds,
inert, leagues still

por andar, levantándose
calcinados, cayéndose
de espaldas, poco dicen.

Diluidos, sin forma
la verdad que en sí ocultan,
huyen de mí los cielos.

Ya en el fin de la Tierra,
sobre el último filo,
resbalando los ojos,

muerta en mí la esperanza,
ese pórtico verde
busco en las negras simas.

¡Oh boquete de sombras!
¡Hervidero del mundo!
¡Qué confusión de siglos!

¡Atrás, atrás! Qué espanto
de tinieblas sin voces!
¡Qué perdida mi alma!

—Ángel muerto, despierta.
¿Dónde estás? Ilumina
con tu rayo el retorno.

Silencio. Más silencio.
Inmóviles los pulsos
del sinfín de la noche.

left to go, they rise,
reduced to ashes, then fall
to their backs, saying little.

Diluted, without form
and hiding a truth within,
the heavens escape me.

Already, at the end of the earth,
at the farthest edge,
the eyes slipping,

hope dying in me,
that green portico
I search for in the black vacuum.

Oh, chasm of shadows!
Hotbed of the world!
What a confusion of centuries!

Back, back! How frightful
the voiceless dark.
How lost, my soul.

Wake up, dead angel.
Where are you? Light
with your ray the return.

Silence. And more silence.
Motionless the pulses
of the endless night.

¡Paraíso perdido!
Perdido por buscarte,
yo, sin luz para siempre.

Paradise lost!
Lost in search of you,
I, without light, forever.

RESIDENT
OF THE MISTS

HUÉSPED
DE LAS NIEBLAS

DESAHUCIO

Ángeles malos o buenos,
que no sé,
te arrojaron en mi alma.

Sola,
sin muebles y sin alcobas,
deshabitada.

De rondón, el viento hiere
las paredes,
las más finas, vítreas láminas.

Humedad. Cadenas. Gritos.
Ráfagas.

Te pregunto:
¿cuándo abandonas la casa,
dime,
qué ángeles malos, crueles,
quieren de nuevo alquilarla?

Dímelo.

EVICTION

Angels, bad or good
I don't know,
flung you into my soul.

Alone,
with neither furniture nor bower,
uninhabited.

Without warning, the wind
bashes the walls,
the finest stained glass.

Humidity. Chains. Hollers.
Squalls.

I ask you:
When you abandon the house,
tell me,
what malevolent angels
will wish to rent it once more?

Tell me.

EL ÁNGEL DESCONOCIDO

¡Nostalgia de los arcángeles!
Yo era . . .
Miradme.

Vestido como en el mundo,
ya no se me ven las alas.
Nadie sabe cómo fui.
No me conocen.

Por las calles, ¿quién se acuerda?
Zapatos son mis sandalias.
Mi túnica, pantalones
y chaqueta inglesa.
Dime quién soy.

Y, sin embargo, yo era . . .

Miradme.

THE OUTSIDER ANGEL

Nostalgia for the archangels!
I was . . .
Look at me.

Dressed as if of this world,
my wings can no longer be seen.
Nobody knows how I was.
They do not know me.

In the streets, who can recall?
Shoes are my sandals.
My tunic, trousers
and an English blazer.
Tell me who I am.

And, nevertheless, I was . . .

Look at me.

EL CUERPO DESHABITADO

1

Yo te arrojé de mi cuerpo,
yo, con un carbón ardiendo.

—Vete.

Madrugada.
La luz, muerta en las esquinas
y en las casas.

Los hombres y las mujeres
ya no estaban.

—Vete.

Quedó mi cuerpo vacío,
negro saco, a la ventana.

Se fue.
Se fue, doblando las calles.
Mi cuerpo anduvo, sin nadie.

THE ABANDONED BODY

1

I threw you off my body,
me, with a burning coal.

Go away!

Daybreak.
Light, dead on the corners
and in the houses.

The men and the women
were no longer there.

Go away!

My body was empty,
black sack at the window.

It left.
It left, rounding the streets.
My body walked, alone.

2

Que cuatro sombras malas
te sacaron en hombros,
muerta.

De mi corazón, muerta,
perforando tus ojos
largas púas de encono
y olvido.

De olvido,
sin posible retorno.
Muerta.

Y entraste tú de pie,
bella.

Entraste tú, y ahora,
por los cielos peores,
tendida,
fea,
sola.

Tú.

Sola entre cuatro sombras.
Muerta.

2

That four bad shadows
took you on their shoulders,
Dead One.

From my heart, Dead One,
stabbing your eyes,
long spikes of rancor
and oblivion.

From oblivion,
without any possible return,
Dead One.

And you entered by foot,
beautiful.

You entered, and now,
through the worst skies,
stretched out,
ugly,
alone.

You.

Alone among four shadows,
Dead One.

3

¿Quién sacude en mi almohada
reinados de yel y sangre,
cielos de azufre,
mares de vinagre?
¿Qué voz difunta los manda?

Contra mí, mundos enteros,
contra mí, dormido,
maniatado,
indefenso.

Nieblas de a pie y a caballo,
nieblas regidas
por humos que yo conozco
en mí enterrados,
van a borrarme.

Y se derrumban murallas,
los fuertes de las ciudades
que me velaban.

Y se derrumban las torres,
las empinadas
centinelas de mi sueño.

Y el viento,
la tierra,
la noche.

3

Who shakes onto my pillow
kingdoms of bile and blood,
sulfur skies,
vinegar seas?
What dead voice commands them?

Against me, entire worlds,
against me, sleeping,
manacled,
defenseless.

Fogs on foot, on horseback,
fogs governed
by the smoke I know,
buried within me,
that will erase me.

And the walls collapse,
the cities' citadels
that kept vigil over me.

And the towers collapse,
steep sentinels
of my dream.

And the wind,
the earth,
the night.

4

Tú. Yo. (Luna.) Al estanque.
Brazos verdes y sombras
te apretaban el talle.

Recuerdo. No recuerdo.
¡Ah, sí! Pasaba un traje
deshabitado, hueco,
cal muerta, entre los árboles.

Yo seguía . . . Dos voces
me dijeron que a nadie.

4

You. Me. (Moon.) By the lake.
Verdant arms and shadows
strangled your waist.

I remember. I don't remember.
Ah, yes! An empty suit
was passing by, holes,
dead lime, among the trees.

I followed . . . Two voices
told me it was no one.

5

Dándose contra los quicios,
contra los árboles.

La luz no le ve, ni el viento,
ni los cristales.
Ya, ni los cristales.

No conoce las ciudades.
No las recuerda.
Va muerto.
Muerto, de pie, por las calles.

No le preguntéis. ¡Prendedle!
No, dejadle.

Sin ojos, sin voz, sin sombra.
Ya, sin sombra.
Invisible para el mundo,
para nadie.

5

Bumping against the doorjambs,
against the trees.

The light does not see him, neither the wind,
neither the crystals.
Yes, not even the crystals.

He does not know the cities.
He does not remember them.
The dead one goes.
The dead one, by foot, through the streets.

Don't interrogate him. Seize him!
No, leave him be.

Sans eyes, sans voice, sans shadow.
Yes, sans shadow.
Invisible to the world,
invisible to anyone.

6

I

Llevaba una ciudad dentro.
La perdió.
Le perdieron.

Solo, en el filo del mundo,
clavado ya, de yeso.

No es un hombre, es un boquete
de humedad, negro,
por el que no se ve nada.

Grito.
¡Nada!

Un boquete, sin eco.

6

I

He carried a city inside him.
He lost it.
They lost him.

Alone, at the edge of the world,
already nailed, already plastered.

He is not a man, he is
a dank ditch, pitch black,
down which nothing can be seen.

A cry.
Nothing!

A ditch, without echo.

7

II

Llevaba una ciudad dentro.
Y la perdió sin combate.
Y le perdieron.

Sombras vienen a llorarla,
a llorarle.

—Tú, caída,
tú, derribada,
tú,
la mejor de las ciudades.

Y tú, muerto,
tú, una cueva,
un pozo tú, seco.

Te dormiste.
Y ángeles turbios, coléricos,
la carbonizaron.
Te carbonizaron tu sueño.

Y ángeles turbios, coléricos,
carbonizaron tu alma,
tu cuerpo.

7

II

He carried a city inside him.
And lost it without a fight.
And they lost him.

Shadows came to mourn it,
to mourn him.

You, fallen one,
you, overthrown,
you,
the greatest of cities.

And you, Dead One,
you, a cave,
you, a dry well.

You slept,
and angels, troubled and choleric,
carbonized it.
Carbonized your dreams.

And angels, troubled and choleric,
carbonized your soul,
your body.

8
(VISITA)

Humo. Niebla. Sin forma,
saliste de mi cuerpo,
funda vacía, sola.

Sin herir los fanales
nocturnos de la alcoba,
por la ciudad del aire.

De la mano del yelo,
las deslumbradas calles,
humo, niebla, te vieron.

Y hundirte en la velada,
fría luz en silencio
de una oculta ventana.

8

(Visitation)

Smoke. Mist. Shapeless,
you left my body
an empty sheath, lonesome.

Without hitting
the nightstand's lights,
out into the city of wind.

Hand in hand with the ice,
unlit streets,
of smoke, of fog, saw you.

And plunged you into evening,
cold light, into the hush
of a hidden window.

EL ÁNGEL BUENO

Un año, ya dormido,
alguien que no esperaba
se paró en mi ventana.

—¡Levántate! Y mis ojos
vieron plumas y espadas.

Atrás, montes y mares,
nubes, picos y alas,
los ocasos, las albas.

—¡Mírala ahí! Su sueño,
pendiente de la nada.

—¡Oh anhelo, fijo mármol,
fija luz, fijas aguas
movibles de mi alma!

Alguien dijo: ¡Levántate!
Y me encontré en tu estancia.

THE GOOD ANGEL

One year, already asleep,
someone I did not expect
stood at my window.

Get up! And my eyes
saw plumes and swords.

Behind those, mountains and seas,
clouds, beaks and wings.
Sunsets, sunrises.

Look at her there! Her dream,
hanging from nothing.

Oh desire, fixed marble,
steady light, steady streaming waters
of my soul!

Someone said: *Get up!*
And I found myself in your room.

MADRIGAL SIN REMEDIO

Porque al fin te perdieron fuegos tristes
   y humos lentos velaron,
vedaron el castillo, nívea cárcel,
donde la rosa olvida sus fantasmas,

mi corazón, sin voz, ni batallones,
   viene solo al asalto
de esas luces, espejos de ceniza,
llevadoras a un muerto sur de muertes.

Ve su pecho ascendido en dos arroyos
   de agua y sangre, hacia el tuyo
quemado ya por huecos tizos fáciles,
falsos, flor, pena mía, sin remedio.

MADRIGAL WITHOUT REDRESS

Because, finally, the sad fires abandoned you
    and the slow smoke watched,
closing off the castle, the snow-covered jail,
where the rose forgets its ghost,

my heart, with neither voice nor battalion,
    comes solo to the bum-rush
of those lights, mirrors of ash,
bearers of a dead one south of death.

See his chest, risen, in two brooks
    of water and blood, toward yours,
already burnt hollow, kindling, facile
and false, flower, my sorrow, without redress.

JUICIO

¡Oh sorpresa de nieve desceñida,
   vigilante, invasora!
Voces veladas, por robar la aurora,
   te llevan detenida.

Ya el fallo de la luz hunde su grito,
   juez de sombra, en tu nada.
(Y en el mundo una estrella fue apagada.
   Otra, en el infinito.)

JUDGMENT

Oh, surprise of fallen snow,
    vigilant, invasive!
Veiled voices, to rob the dawn . . .
    they take you prisoner.

Already the verdict of light sinks its cry,
    shadow judge, in your nothingness.
(And in the world a star was extinguished.
    Another, in the infinite.)

LOS ÁNGELES BÉLICOS

(Norte, Sur)

Viento contra viento.
Yo, torre sin mando, en medio.

Remolinos de ciudades
bajan los desfiladeros.
Ciudades del viento sur,
que me vieron.

Por las neveras, rodando,
pueblos.
Pueblos que yo desconozco,
ciudades del viento norte,
que no me vieron.

Gentío de mar y tierra,
nombres, preguntas, recuerdos,
frente a frente.
Balumbas de frío encono,
cuerpo a cuerpo.

Yo, torre sin mando, en medio,
livida torre colgada
de almas muertas que me vieron,
que no me vieron.

Viento contra viento.

WAR ANGELS
(North, South)

Wind against wind.
I, unfettered tower, in the middle.

Whirlwinds of cities
go down the gorges.
Cities of the south wind,
who saw me.

By the rolling snowfields,
villages.
Villages I don't know,
cities of the north wind,
who did not see me.

Horde of sea and soil,
names, questions, memories,
face to face.
Heaps of bitter cold,
body to body.

I, unfettered tower, in the middle,
raging tower hung
with dead spirits who saw me,
who did not see me.

Wind against wind.

EL ÁNGEL DE LOS NÚMEROS

Vírgenes con esquadras
y compases, velando
las celestes pizarras.

Y el ángel de los números,
pensativo, volando
del 1 al 2, del 2
al 3, del 3 al 4.

Tizas frías y esponjas
rayaban y borraban
la luz de los espacios.

Ni sol, luna, ni estrellas,
ni el repentino verde
del rayo y el relámpago,
ni el aire. Sólo nieblas.

Vírgenes sin esquadras,
sin compases, llorando.

Y en las muertas pizarras,
el ángel de los números,
sin vida, amortajado
sobre el 1 y el 2,
sobre el 3, sobre el 4 . . .

THE ANGEL OF NUMBERS

Virgins with squares
and compasses, watching
the celestial blackboards.

And the angel of numbers,
pensive, flying
from 1 to 2, from 2
to 3, from 3 to 4.

Cold chalk and sponges
scratch out and erase
the light from the lecture halls.

Not the sun or the moon, not the stars,
not the sudden green
of the lightning's bolt and flash,
not the air. Only mist.

Virgins without squares,
without compasses, crying.

And on the dead blackboards,
the angel of numbers,
lifeless, shrouded
above the 1 and the 2,
above the 3, above the 4 . . .

CANCIÓN DEL ÁNGEL SIN SUERTE

Tú eres lo que va:
agua que me lleva,
que me dejará.

Buscadme en la ola.

Lo que va y no vuelve:
viento que en la sombra
se apaga y se enciende.

Buscadme en la nieve.

Lo que nadie sabe:
tierra movediza
que no habla con nadie.

Buscadme en el aire.

SONG OF THE LUCKLESS ANGEL

You are what goes:
water that delivers me,
water that leaves me behind.

Look for me in the wave.

What goes and does not come back:
wind that, in the shade,
gives out then ignites.

Look for me in the snow.

What nobody knows:
tremulous earth
that speaks to nobody.

Look for me in the air.

EL ÁNGEL DESENGAÑADO

Quemando los fríos,
tu voz prendió en mí:
ven a mi país.

Te esperan ciudades,
sin vivos ni muertos,
para coronarte.

—Me duermo.
No me espera nadie.

THE DISILLUSIONED ANGEL

Burning the cold,
your voice caught hold of me:
Come to my country.

Cities await you,
sans the living, sans the dead,
to crown you.

—I am sleeping.
No one awaits me.

EL ÁNGEL MENTIROSO

Y fui derrotada
yo, sin violencia,
con miel y palabras.

Y, sola, en provincias
de arena y de viento,
sin hombre, cautiva.

Y, sombra de alguien,
cien puertas de siglos
tapiaron mi sangre.

¡Ay luces! ¡Conmigo!

Que fui derrotada
yo, sin violencia,
con miel y palabras.

THE LYING ANGEL

And I was defeated,
I, without violence,
with honey and words.

And, alone, in provinces
of sand and wind,
solitary, captive.

And, someone's shadow,
one hundred gates of centuries
dammed my blood.

Oh, lights! With me!

For I was defeated,
I, without violence,
with honey and words.

INVITACIÓN AL AIRE

Te invito, sombra, al aire.
Sombra de veinte siglos,
a la verdad del aire,
del aire, aire, aire.

Sombra que nunca sales
de tu cueva, y al mundo
no devolviste el silbo
que al nacer te dio el aire,
el aire, aire, aire.

Sombra sin luz, minera
por las profundidades
de veinte tumbas, veinte
siglos huecos sin aire,
sin aire, aire, aire.

¡Sombra, a los picos, sombra,
de la verdad del aire,
del aire, aire, aire!

INVITATION TO THE AIR

I invite you, shadow, to the air.
Shadow of twenty centuries,
to the truth of the air,
of the air, air, air.

Shadow that never exits
your cave, and to the world
never gave back the whistle
that, at birth, gave you the air,
the air, air, air.

Shadow sans light, mining
the depths
of twenty tombs, twenty
centuries, empty and without air,
without air, air, air.

Shadow, to the summits, shadow,
of the truth of the air,
of the air, air, air.

LOS ÁNGELES MOHOSOS

Hubo luz que trajo
por hueso una almendra amarga.

Voz que por sonido,
el fleco de la lluvia,
cortado por un hacha.

Alma que por cuerpo,
la funda de aire
de una doble espada.

Venas que por sangre,
yel de mirra y de retama.

Cuerpo que por alma,
el vacío, nada.

THE RANCID ANGELS

There was a light that brought
for bone a bitter almond.

Voice that for sound,
the fringe of rain,
chopped by an axe.

Soul that for body,
the wind scabbard
of a double-edged sword.

Veins that for blood,
the bile of broom and myrrh.

Body that for soul,
the void, the nothing.

EL ÁNGEL CENICIENTO

Precipitadas las luces
por los derrumbos del cielo,
en la barca de las nieblas
bajaste tú, Ceniciento.

Para romper cadenas
y enfrentar a la tierra contra el viento.

Iracundo, ciego.

Para romper cadenas
y enfrentar a los mares contra el fuego.

Dando bandazos el mundo,
por la nada rodó, muerto.
No se enteraron los hombres.
Sólo tú y yo, Ceniciento.

THE ASHEN ANGEL

Lights precipitated
by the sky's collapse,
in the ferry of fog
you came down, Ashen One.

To break chains
and pit earth against wind.

Wrathful, blind.

To break chains
and pit seas against fire.

The world lurching,
rolled into the nothing, dead.
The men had not heard.
Only you and I, Ashen One.

EL ÁNGEL RABIOSO

Son puertas de sangre,
        milenios de odios,
lluvias de rencores, mares.

        ¿Qué te hice, dime,
        para que los saltes?
¿Para que con tu agrio aliento
me incendies todos mis ángeles?

        Hachas y relámpagos
        de poco me valen.

Noches armadas, ni vientos
        leales.

        Rompes y me asaltas.
        Cautivo me traes
a tu luz, que no es la mía,
        para tornearme.

A tu luz agria, tan agria,
        que no muerde nadie.

THE RAGING ANGEL

There are doors of blood,
millenia of hatreds,
rains of rancor, seas.

      What have I done to you, tell me,
      so you can move past it?
So that with your acrid breath
you set fire to all my angels?

      Hatchets and flashes of lightning
      are of little value to me.

Neither armed nights nor faithful
winds.

      You break and assault me.
      Captive, you take me
to your light, which is not my own,
      in order to turn me.

To your acrid light, so acrid
      that nobody bites.

EL ÁNGEL BUENO

Dentro del pecho se abren
corredores anchos, largos,
que sorben todas las mares.

Vidrieras,
que alumbran todas las calles.

Miradores,
que acercan todas las torres.

Ciudades deshabitadas
se pueblan, de pronto. Trenes
descarrilados, unidos
marchan.

Naufragios antiguos flotan.
La luz moja el pie en el agua.

¡Campanas!

Gira más de prisa el aire.
El mundo, con ser el mundo,
en la mano de una niña cabe.

¡Campanas!

Una carta del cielo bajó un ángel.

THE GOOD ANGEL

Inside the chest open
wide, long corridors
that soak up all the seas.

Windows,
that illuminate all streets.

Balconies,
that draw near all towers.

Abandoned cities
suddenly populate. Trains,
derailed then rejoined,
ramble forth.

Ancient shipwrecks float.
Light dips its foot in the water.

Bells!

The wind spins faster.
The world, being the world,
fits into the palm of a girl.

Bells!

A letter from heaven brought down by an angel.

RESIDENT
OF THE MISTS

HUÉSPED
DE LAS NIEBLAS

LOS DOS ÁNGELES

Ángel de luz, ardiendo,
¡oh, ven!, y con tu espada
incendia los abismos donde yace
mi subterráneo ángel de las nieblas.

¡Oh espadazo en las sombras!
Chispas múltiples,
clavándose en mi cuerpo,
en mis alas sin plumas,
en lo que nadie ve,
vida.

Me estás quemando vivo.
Vuela ya de mí, oscuro
Luzbel de las canteras sin auroras,
de los pozos sin agua,
de las simas sin sueño,
ya carbón del espíritu,
sol, luna.

Me duelen los cabellos.
y las ansias. ¡Oh, quémame!
¡Más, más, sí, más! Quémame!

¡Quémalo, ángel de luz, custodio mío,
tú que andabas llorando por las nubes,
tú, sin mí, tú, por mí,

THE TWO ANGELS

Angel of light, burning,
oh, come! And with your sword
set fire to the chasms where lies
my subterranean angel of the mists.

Oh, sword clash in the shadows!
Multiple sparks
digging into my body,
into my featherless wings,
into what nobody sees,
life.

You are burning me alive.
Fly away from me, dark
Lucifer of quarries sans daybreak,
of waterless wells,
of sleepless chasms,
coal, already, of the spirit,
sun, moon.

My hair hurts.
And my urges. Oh, burn me!
More, more! Yes, more! Burn me!

Burn it, angel of light, my protector,
you who went crying through the clouds,
you, without me, you, for me,

ángel frío de polvo, ya sin gloria,
volcado en las tinieblas!

¡Quémalo, ángel de luz,
quémame y huye!

cold angel of dust, now without glory,
overthrown in the dark!

Burn it down, angel of light,
burn me and fly away!

5

Cinco manos de ceniza
quemando la bruma, abriendo
cinco vías
para el agua turbia,
para el turbio viento.

Te buscan vivo.
Y no te encuentran.
Te buscan muerto.
No muerto, dormido.
Y sí.

Y sí, porque cinco manos
cayeron sobre tu cuerpo
cuando inmóvil resbalaba
sobre los cinco navegables ríos
que dan almas corrientes, voz al sueño.

Y no viste.
Era su luz la que cayó primero.
Mírala, seca, en el suelo.

Y no oíste.
Era su voz la que alargada hirieron.
Óyela muda, en el eco.

Y no oliste.
Era su esencia la que hendió el silencio.
Huélela fría, en el viento.

5

Five hands of ash
burning the mist, opening
five roads
for troubled water,
for troubled wind.

They look for you alive.
And do not find you.
They look for you dead.
Not dead, asleep.
And yes.

And yes, because five hands
fell upon your body
when, immobile, it slipped
on the five navigable rivers
that give common souls voice to dream.

And you did not see.
It was his light that fell first.
Look at it, barren, on the earth.

And you did not hear.
It was his voice, drawn out, that they bruised.
Hear it, silent, in the echo.

And you did not smell.
It was his essence that cracked the quiet.
Smell it, cold, on the wind.

Y no gustaste.
Era su nombre el que rodó deshecho.
Gústalo en tu lengua, muerto.

Y no tocaste.
El desaparecido era su cuerpo.
Tócalo en la nada, yelo.

And you did not taste.
It was his name that came undone.
Taste it, Dead One, on your tongue.

And you did not touch.
The disappeared was his body.
Touch it in the nothingness, ice.

LOS ÁNGELES DE LA PRISA

Espíritus de seis alas,
seis espíritus pajizos,
me empujaban.

Seis ascuas.

Acelerado aire era mi sueño
por las aparecidas esperanzas
de los rápidos giros de los cielos,
de los veloces, espirales pueblos,
rodadoras montañas,
raudos mares, riberas, ríos, yermos.

Me empujaban.

Enemiga era la tierra,
porque huía.
Enemigo el cielo,
porque no paraba.
Y tú, mar,
y tú, fuego,
y tú,
acelerado aire de mi sueño.

Seis ascuas,
oculto el nombre y las caras,
empujándome de prisa.

HASTY ANGELS

Six-winged spirits,
six straw spirits,
pushed me.

Six embers.

Accelerated wind was my dream
for the emerging hopes
of the quick spinning of the skies,
of the speedy, spiraling villages,
somersaulting mountains,
swift seas, shores, rivers, wastelands.

They pushed me.

The enemy was the earth,
because it escaped.
Enemy the sky,
because it did not stop.
And you, sea,
and you, fire,
and you,
accelerated wind of my dream.

Six embers,
hiding the name and the faces,
pushing me, rushed.

¡Paradme!
Nada.
¡Paradme todo, un momento!
Nada.

No querían
que yo me parara en nada.

Stop me!
Nothing.
Stop me forever, for a moment!
Nothing.

They did not want me
to stop at anything.

LOS ÁNGELES CRUELES

Pájaros, ciegos los picos
de aquel tiempo.
Perforados,
por un rojo alambre en celo,
la voz y los albedríos,
largos, cortos, de sus sueños:
la mar, los campos, las nubes,
el árbol, el arbolillo . . .
Ciegos, muertos.

¡Volad!
—No Podemos.
¿Cómo quieres que volemos?

Jardines que eran el aire
de aquel tiempo.
Cañas de la ira nocturna,
espolazos de los torpes,
turbios vientos,
que quieren ser hojas, flor,
que quieren . . .

¡Jardines del sur, deshechos!
Del sur, muertos.

¡Airead!
—No Podemos.
¿Cómo quieres que aireemos?

THE CRUEL ANGELS

Birds, blind the beaks
of that far-off time.
Punctured
by a red hot wire,
the voice and the whims,
long, short, of their dreams:
the sea, the open fields, the clouds,
the tree, the seedling . . .
Blind, dead.

Take wing!
We can't.
How do you want us to fly?

Gardens that were the air
of that far-off time.
Canes of nocturnal rage,
spurs of the rough,
troubled winds,
that want to be leaves, flower,
that want . . .

Gardens of the south, undone!
Of the south, dead.

Up with you!
We can't.
How do you want us to rise?

En tus manos,
aún calientes, de aquel tiempo,
alas y hojas difuntas.

Enterremos.

In your hands,
still warm, from that far off time,
wings and dead leaves.

Let us bury them.

EL ÁNGEL ÁNGEL

Y el mar fue y le dio un nombre
y un apellido el viento
y las nubes un cuerpo
y un alma el fuego.

La tierra, nada.

Ese reino movible,
colgado de las águilas,
no la conoce.

Nunca escribió su sombra
la figura de un hombre.

THE ANGEL ANGEL

And the sea went and gave her a name
and a surname, the wind,
and the clouds a body,
and a soul, fire.

The earth, nothing.

That moveable kingdom,
hanging from eagles,
does not know her.

Her shadow never chalked
the outline of a man.

ENGAÑO

Alguien detrás, a tu espalda
tapándote los ojos con palabras.

Detrás de ti, sin cuerpo,
sin alma.
Ahumada voz de sueño
cortado.
Ahumada voz
cortada.

Con palabras, vidrios falsos.

Ciega, por un túnel de oro,
de espejos malos,
con la muerte
darás en un subterráneo.

Tú allí sola, con la muerte,
en un subterráneo.

Y alguien detrás, a tu espalda,
siempre.

DECEPTION

Someone behind your back,
blindfolding you with words.

Behind you, without a body,
without a soul.
Smoke-tinged voice
of a dream cut short.
Smoke-tinged voice,
cut short.

With words, fake panes of glass.

Blind, down a tunnel of gold,
of mischievous mirrors,
with death
you will stumble upon a passage.

You there, alone with death,
in an underground passage.

And someone behind your back,
always.

EL ÁNGEL DE CARBÓN

Feo, de hollín y fango.
¡No verte!

Antes, de nieve, áureo,
en trineo por mi alma.
Cuajados pinos. Pendientes.

Y ahora por las cocheras,
de carbón, sucio.
¡Te lleven!

Por los desvanes de los sueños rotos.
Telarañas. Polillas. Polvo.
¡Te condenen!

Tiznados por tus manos,
mis muebles, mis paredes.

En todo,
tu estampado recuerdo
de tinta negra y barro.
¡Te quemen!

Amor, pulpo de sombra,
malo.

THE ANGEL OF COAL

Ugly, of soot and silt.
I do not see you!

Before, of snow, golden,
sledding toward my soul.
Congealed pines. Slopes.

And now, via dirty depots
of coal.
Away with you!

Through the attics of broken dreams.
Cobwebs. Moths. Dust.
Damn you!

Stained by your hands,
my furniture, my walls.

On everything,
your memory stamped
in black, in sludge.
Burn!

Love, octopus of shadow,
wretched.

EL ÁNGEL DE LA IRA

Sin dueño, entre las ortigas,
piedra por pulir, brillabas.

Pie invisible.
(Entre las ortigas, nada.)
Pie invisible de la ira.

Lenguas de légamo, hundidas,
sordas, recordaron algo.

Ya no estabas.
¿Qué recordaron?

Se movió mudo el silencio
y dijo algo.
No dijo nada.

Sin saberlo,
mudó de rumbo mi sangre,
y en los fosos
gritos largos se cayeron.

Para salvar mis ojos,
para salvarte a ti que . . .

Secreto.

THE ANGEL OF ANGER

Without a lord, among the nettles.
Grindstone, you gleamed.

Invisible foot.
(Among the nettles, nothing.)
Invisible foot of fury.

Tongues of sludge, submerged,
deaf, remembered something.

You were gone.
What did they remember?

The silence moved, mute,
and said something.
Said nothing.

Without knowing it,
my blood changed course,
and into the trenches
long hollers fell.

To save my eyes,
to save you who . . .

Secret.

EL ÁNGEL ENVIDIOSO

Leñadoras son, ¡defiéndete!,
esas silbadoras hachas
que mueven mi lengua.

Hoces de los vientos malos,
¡alerta!,
que muerden mi alma.

Torre de desconfianza,
tú.

Tú, torre dele oro, avara.
Ciega las ventanas.

O no, mira.

Hombres arrasados, fijos,
por las ciudades taladas.
Pregúntales.

O no, escucha.

Un cielo, verde de envidia,
rebosa mi boca y canta.

Yo, un cielo . . .

Ni escuches ni mires. Yo . . .
Ciega las ventanas.

THE ENVIOUS ANGEL

There be lumberjacks. Defend yourself!
Those whistling hatchets
that stir my tongue.

Sickles of the bad winds—
Alert!—that bite
into my soul.

Tower of distrust,
you.

You, greedy tower of gold.
Blind your windows.

Oh no, look.

Men laid waste, for good,
in the felled cities.
Ask them.

Oh no, listen.

A sky, green with envy,
spills from my mouth and sings.

I, a sky . . .

Neither listen nor look. I . . .
Blind your windows.

LOS ÁNGELES VENGATIVOS

No, no te conocieron
las almas conocidas.
Sí la mía.

¿Quién eres tú, dinos, que no te recordamos
ni de la tierra ni del cielo?

Tu sombra, dinos, ¿de qué espacio?
¿Qué luz la prolongó, habla,
hasta nuestro reinado?

¿De dónde vienes, dinos,
sombra sin palabras,
que no te recordamos?
¿Quién te manda?
Si relámpago fuiste en algún sueño,
relámpagos se olvidan, apagados.

Y por desconocida,
las almas conocidas te mataron.
No la mía.

THE VENGEFUL ANGELS

No, the known souls
did not know you.
Mine did.

Who are you, tell us, who do not remember you
from earth or from heaven?

Your shadow—tell us—is from what space?
What light, say it, has reached
into our realm?

Where do you come from, tell us,
shadow without words,
that we don't remember you?
Who sent you?
If you were lightning in a dream,
lightning is forgotten, doused.

And for being unknown,
the known souls murdered you.
Not mine.

CAN DE LLAMAS

Sur.
Campo metálico, seco.
Plano, sin alma, mi cuerpo.

Centro.
Grande, tapándolo todo,
la sombra fija del perro.

Norte.
Espiral sola mi alma,
jaula buscando a su sueño.

¡Salta sobre los dos! ¡Hiérelos!
¡Sombra del can, fija, salta!
¡Únelos, sombra del perro!

Riegan los aires aullidos
dentados de agudos fuegos.

¡Norte!
Se agiganta el viento norte . . .
Y huye el alma.

¡Sur!
Se agiganta el viento sur . . .
Y huye el cuerpo.

¡Centro!
Y huye, centro,

HOUND OF FLAMES

South.
Metallic field, barren.
Plain, soulless, my body.

Center.
Vast, blanketing everything,
the petrified shadow of the dog.

North.
Spiral solo my soul,
jail cell in search of its dream.

Leap over both! Hurt them!
Shadow of the hound, petrified, leap!
Unite them, dog shadow!

Jagged howls of high flames
saturate the air.

North!
The north wind swells . . .
and the soul escapes.

South!
The south wind swells . . .
and the body escapes.

Center!
And the center escapes,

candente, intensa, infinita,
la sombra inmóvil del perro.
Su sombra fija.

Campo metálico, seco.
Sin nadie.
Seco.

incandescent, intense, infinite,
the static shadow of the dog.
His petrified shadow.

Metallic field, barren.
Desolate.
Bone-dry.

EL ÁNGEL TONTO

Ese ángel,
ése que niega el limbo de su fotografía
y hace pájaro muerto
su mano.

Ese ángel que teme que le pidan las alas,
que le besen el pico,
seriamente,
sin contrato.

Si es del cielo y tan tonto,
¿por qué en la tierra? Dime.
Decidme.

No en las calles, en todo,
indiferente, necio,
me lo encuentro.

¡El ángel tonto!

¡Si será de la tierra!
—Sí, de la tierra solo.

THE FOOLISH ANGEL

That angel,
that one who denies the limbo of his photograph
and makes a dead bird
of his hands.

That angel who fears they will ask for his wings,
that they will kiss his beak,
seriously,
without a contract.

If he is from heaven and so foolish,
why is he on earth? Tell me.
Tell me.

Not in the streets, but everywhere,
indifferent, foolish,
I find him.

The foolish angel!

He will be of the earth!
Yes, of the earth alone.

EL ÁNGEL DEL MISTERIO

Un sueño sin faroles y una humedad de olvidos,
pisados por un nombre y una sombra.
No sé si por un nombre o muchos nombres,
si por una sombra o muchas sombras.
Reveládmelo.

Sé que habitan los pozos frías voces,
que son de un solo cuerpo o muchos cuerpos,
de un alma sola o muchas almas.
No sé.
Decídmelo.

Que un caballo sin nadie va estampando
a su amazona antigua por los muros.
Que en las almenas grita, muerto, alguien
que yo toqué, dormido, en un espejo,
que yo, mudo, le dije . . .
No sé.
Explicádmelo.

THE ANGEL OF MYSTERY

A dream without lanterns and a dank forgetfulness,
trampled by a name and a shadow.
I don't know whether by one name or many names,
whether by one shadow or many shadows.
Reveal it to me.

I know that cold voices inhabit the wells,
that they are of a single body or of many bodies,
of a single soul or of many souls.
I don't know.
Tell me.

That a horse with no rider goes stamping
its old equestrian to the walls.
That on the parapet hollers, dead, someone
that I touched, asleep, in a mirror,
that I, mute, said to him . . .
I don't know.
Make it plain for me.

ASCENSIÓN

Azotando, hiriendo las paredes, las humedades,
se oyeron silbar cuerdas,
alargadas preguntas entre los musgos y la oscuridad colgante.
Se oyeron.
Las oíste.

Garfios mudos buceaban
el silencio estirado del agua, buscándote.
Tumba rota,
el silencio estirado del agua.
Y cuatro boquetes, buscándote.

Ecos de alma hundida en un sueño moribundo,
de alma que ya no tiene que perder tierras ni mares,
cuatro ecos, arriba, escapándose.

A la luz,
a los cielos,
a los aires.

ASCENSION

Whipping, wounding the walls, wounding the dank,
ropes were heard whistling,
stretching questions between moss and the hanging dark.
They were heard.
You heard them.

Mute hooks dredged
the stretched silence of the blue, in search of you.
Broken sepulcher,
the stretched silence of the blue.
And four chasms, in search of you.

Echoes of a soul sunk in a dying dream,
of a soul that no longer has lands or seas to lose,
four echoes, above, escaping.

To the light,
to the skies,
to the air.

LOS ÁNGELES MUDOS

Inmóviles, clavadas, mudas mujeres de los zaguanes
y hombres sin voz, lentos, de las bodegas,
quieren, quisieran, querrían preguntarme:
—¿Cómo tú por aquí y en otra parte?

Querrían hombres, mujeres, mudos, tocarme,
saber si mi sombra, si mi cuerpo andan sin alma
por otras calles.
Quisieran decirme:
—Si eres tú, párate.

Hombres, mujeres, mudos, querrían ver claro,
asomarse a mi alma,
acercarle una cerilla
por ver si es la misma.
Quieren, quisieran . . .
—Habla.

Y van a morirse, mudos,
sin saber nada.

THE MUTE ANGELS

Stone still, riveted, mute women from the corridors,
and slow, voiceless men, from the storehouses,
they want, they would want . . . that is, they would like . . . to ask me:
How are you here and elsewhere?

Mute men, mute women, would like to touch me,
to know if my shadow, if my body walks without a soul
down other streets.
They would like to tell me:
If it is you, stop.

Mute men, mute women, would like to see clearly,
peer into my soul,
bring a match to it,
to see if it's the same.
They want, they may want . . .
Speak.

And they will die, mute,
knowing nothing.

EL ALMA EN PENA

Esa alma en pena, sola,
esa alma en pena siempre perseguida
por un resplandor muerto.
Por un muerto.

Cerrojos, llaves, puertas
saltan a deshora
y cortinas heladas en la noche se alargan,
se estiran,
se incendian,
se prolongan.

Te conozco,
te recuerdo,
bujía inerte, lívido halo, nimbo difunto,
te conozco aunque ataques diluido en el viento.

Párpados desvelados
vienen a tierra.
Sísmicos latigazos tumban sueños,
terremotos derriban las estrellas.
Catástrofes celestes tiran al mundo escombros,
alas rotas, laúdes, cuerdas de arpas,
restos de ángeles.

No hay entrada en el cielo para nadie.

En pena, siempre en pena,
alma perseguida.

THE SOUL IN PAIN

That soul in pain, alone,
that soul in pain, always persecuted
by a dead blaze.
By a Dead One.

Deadbolts, keys, doors
jump at some ungodly hour
and, each night, icy drapes reach out,
they stretch,
catch fire,
and stretch some more.

I know you,
I remember you,
idle candle, livid halo, dead nimbus,
I know you, though dilated, attacking in the wind.

Unveiled eyelids
come to earth.
Seismic lashes lay waste to dreams,
earthquakes bring down stars.
Celestial catastrophes throw rubble on the world,
broken wings, lutes, harp strings,
remains of angels.

There is no entry into heaven for anyone.

In pain, always in pain,
persecuted soul.

A contraluz siempre,
nunca alcanzada, sola,
alma sola.

Aves contra barcos,
hombres contra rosas,
las perdidas batallas en los trigos,
la explosión de la sangre en las olas.
Y el fuego.
El fuego muerto,
el resplandor sin vida,
siempre vigilante en la sombra.

Alma en pena:
el resplandor sin vida,
tu derrota.

Backlit always,
never attained, alone,
soul alone.

Birds against boats,
men against roses,
the lost battles in the buckwheat,
the explosion of blood in the waves.
And the fire.
The dead fire,
the lifeless blaze,
always vigilant in the shadow.

Soul in pain:
the lifeless blaze
you slaughter.

EL ÁNGEL BUENO

Vino el que yo quería,
el que yo llamaba.

No aquel que barre cielos sin defensas,
luceros sin cabañas,
lunas sin patria,
nieves.
Nieves de esas caídas de una mano,
un nombre,
un sueño,
una frente.

No aquel que a sus cabellos
ató la muerte.

El que yo quería.

Sin arañar los aires,
sin herir hojas ni mover cristales.

Aquel que a sus cabellos
ató el silencio.

Para, sin lastimarme,
cavar una ribera de luz dulce en mi pecho
y hacerme el alma navegable.

THE GOOD ANGEL

The one I wanted came,
the one I called.

Not the one who rakes defenseless skies,
stars unhoused,
moons in exile,
snows.
Snows like those that fell from a hand,
a name,
a dream,
a brow.

Not the one who tied their hair
to death.

The one I wanted.

Without scratching the wind,
without hurting leaves or shifting crystals.

The one who tied their hair
to silence.

To, without hurting myself, dredge
a river's edge of sweet light into my chest
and make my soul traversable.

EL ÁNGEL AVARO

Gentes de la esquinas
de pueblos y naciones que no están en el mapa,
comentaban.

Ese hombre está muerto
y no lo sabe.
Quiere asaltar la banca,
robar nubes, estrellas, cometas de oro,
comprar lo más difícil:
el cielo.
Y ese hombre está muerto.

Temblores subterráneos le sacuden la frente.
Tumbos de tierra desprendida,
ecos desvariados,
sones confusos de piquetas y azadas,
los oídos.
Los ojos,
luces de acetileno,
húmedas, áureas galerías.
El corazón,
explosiones de piedras, júbilos, dinamita.

Sueña con las minas.

THE GREEDY ANGEL

Street corner people
from towns and nations of no map,
remarked.

That man is dead
and doesn't know it.
He wants to rob the bank,
steal clouds, stars, comets of gold,
buy what's most difficult:
the sky.
And that man is dead.

Subterranean tremors rattle the brow.
Avalanching debris,
wild echoes,
bedlam of pickaxes and hoes,
the ears.
The eyes,
acetylene lights,
humid, golden galleries.
The heart,
explosions of stones, jubilations, dynamite.

Dream of mines.

LOS ÁNGELES SONÁMBULOS

1

Pensad en aquella hora:
cuando se rebelaron contra un rey en tinieblas
los ojos invisibles de las alcobas.

Lo sabéis, lo sabéis. ¡Dejadme!
Si a lo largo de mí se abren grietas de nieve,
tumbas de aguas paradas,
nebulosas de sueños oxidados,
echad la llave para siempre a vuestros párpados.
¿Qué queréis?

Ojos invisibles, grandes, atacan.
Púas incandescentes se hunden en los tabiques.
Ruedan pupilas muertas,
sábanas.

Un rey es un erizo de pestañas.

2

También,
también los oídos invisibles de las alcobas,
contra un rey en tinieblas.

Ya sabéis que mi boca es un pozo de nombres,
de números y letras difuntos.

THE SLEEPWALKING ANGELS

1

Think of that hour:
when the invisible eyes of the bedrooms
rebelled against a king in the dark.

You know it, you know it. Leave me be!
If cracks of snow open along my body,
tombs of stagnant waters,
nebulae of rusted dreams,
lock your eyelids forever.
What is it that you want?

Large, invisible eyes attack.
Incandescent barbs sink into the walls.
Dead pupils dilate,
bed linen.

A king is a hedgehog of eyelashes.

2

Also,
also the invisible ears of the bedrooms,
against a king in the dark.

You already know that my mouth is a well of names,
of dead numbers and letters.

Que los ecos se hastían sin mis palabras
y lo que jamás dije desprecia y odia al viento.

Nada tenéis que oír.
¡Dejadme!

Pero oídos se agrandan contra el pecho.
De escayola, fríos,
bajan a la garganta,
a los sótanos lentos de la sangre,
a los tubos de los huesos.

Un rey es un erizo sin secreto.

That the echoes fatigued without my words
and what I never said despises the wind.

You have nothing to hear.
Leave me be!

But ears grow large against the chest.
Cast in plaster, cold,
they go down the throat,
into the slow cellars of the blood,
through the tubes of the bones.

A king is a hedgehog without a secret.

RESIDENT
OF THE MISTS

HUÉSPED
DE LAS NIEBLAS

TRES RECUERDOS DEL CIELO

Homenaje a Gustavo Adolfo Bécquer

No habían cumplido años ni la rosa ni el arcángel.
Todo, anterior al balido y al llanto.
Cuando la luz ignoraba todavía
si el mar nacería niño o niña.
Cuando el viento soñaba melenas que peinar
y claveles el fuego que encender y mejillas
y el agua unos labios parados donde beber.
Todo, anterior al cuerpo, al nombre y al tiempo.

Entonces, yo recuerdo que, una vez, en el cielo . . .

PRIMER RECUERDO

. . . una azucena tronchada . . .

G.A. Bécquer

Paseaba con un dejo de azucena que piensa,
casi de pájaro que sabe ha de nacer.
Mirándose sin verse a una luna que le hacía espejo el sueño
y a un silencio de nieve, que le elevaba los pies.
A un silencio asomada.
Era anterior al arpa, a la lluvia y a las palabras.
No sabía.
Blanca alumna del aire,
temblaba con las estrellas, con la flor y los árboles.
Su tallo, su verde talle.

THREE MEMORIES OF HEAVEN

Homage to Gustavo Adolfo Bécquer

PROLOGUE

Neither the rose nor the archangel had had a birthday.
Everything, before the bleating and the crying.
When the light was still ignorant
as to whether the sea would be born boy or girl.
When the wind was dreaming of locks to comb
and carnations of fires to set, and cheeks
and water, lips pausing long enough to drink.
Everything, before the body, name, and time.

Then, I remember that, once, in heaven . . .

FIRST MEMORY

. . . a broken lily . . .
G.A. Bécquer

She was strolling with a touch of the thinking lily,
almost like a bird that knows its way to being born.
Looking at herself without seeing a moon that mirrored her sleep
and a snowy silence that caused her to levitate.
To a peeking silence.
It was before the harp, before rain and words.
She did not know.
White schoolgirl of the air,
she trembled with the stars, with the flowers and the trees.
Her stalk, her green figure.

Con las estrellas mías
que, ignorantes de todo,
por cavar dos lagunas en sus ojos
la ahogaron en dos mares.

Y recuerdo . . .

Nada más: muerta, alejarse.

SEGUNDO RECUERDO

> *. . . rumor de besos y batir de alas . . .*
> G.A. Bécquer

También antes,
mucho antes de la rebelión de las sombras,
de que al mundo cayeran plumas incendiadas
y un pájaro pudiera ser muerto por un lirio.
Antes, antes que tú me preguntaras
el número y el sitio de mi cuerpo.
Mucho antes del cuerpo.
En la época del alma.
Cuando tú abriste en la frente sin corona, del cielo,
la primera dinastía del sueño.
Cuando tú, al mirarme en la nada,
investate la primera palabra.

Entonces, nuestro encuentro.

With my stars
that, ignorant of everything,
in digging two lagoons in her eyes,
drowned her in two seas.

And I remember . . .

Nothing more: Dead One, walk away.

SECOND MEMORY

> *. . . rumor of kisses and the flapping of wings . . .*
> G.A. Bécquer

Also before,
long before the shadows' rebellion,
when burning feathers fell onto the world
and a bird could be killed by a lily.
Before, before you could ask me
the number and site of my body.
Long before the body.
In the epoch of the soul.
When you opened upon the crownless forehead, from heaven,
the first dynasty of sleep.
When you, spotting me in the void,
invented the first word.

Then, our encounter.

. . . detrás del abanico
de plumas de oro . . .

G.A. Bécquer

Aún los valses del cielo no habían desposado al jazmín y la nieve,
ni los aires pensado en la posible música de tus cabellos,
ni decretado el rey que la violeta se enterrara en un libro.
No.
Era la era en que la golondrina viajaba
sin nuestras iniciales en el pico.
En que las campanillas y las enredaderas
morían sin balcones que escalar y estrellas.
La era
en que al hombro de un ave no había flor que apoyara la cabeza.

Entonces, detrás de tu abanico, nuestra luna primera.

THIRD MEMORY

> *. . . behind the fan*
> *of gold feathers . . .*
>   G.A. Bécquer

Even heaven's waltzes had not married jasmine to the snow,
nor had the winds thought of the possible song of your hair,
nor had the king decreed that the violet be buried in a book.
No.
It was the age in which the woodswallow travelled
without our initials in its beak.
In which the bluebells and vines
died with neither balconies to climb nor stars.
The era
in which, on the shoulder of a bird, there was no flower to support the head.

Then, behind your fan, our first moon.

EL ÁNGEL DE ARENA

Seriamente, en tus ojos era la mar dos niños que me espiaban,
temerosos de lazos y palabras duras.
Dos niños de la noche, terribles, expulsados del cielo,
cuya infancia era un robo de barcos y un crimen de soles y de lunas.
Duérmete. Ciérralos.

Vi que el mar verdadero era un muchacho que saltaba desnudo,
invitándome a un plato de estrellas y a un reposo de algas.
¡Sí, sí! Ya mi vida iba a ser, ya lo era, litoral desprendido.
Pero tú, despertando, me hundiste en tus ojos.

THE ANGEL OF SAND

Seriously, in your eyes the sea was two children spying on me,
afraid of knots and harsh words.
Two children of the night, terrible, expelled from heaven,
whose childhood was a robbery of ships and a crime of suns and moons.
Sleep now. Close your eyes.

I saw that the true sea was a boy who jumped naked,
inviting me to a plate of stars and a bed of algae.
Yes, yes! My life would be, already was, a detached coast.
But you, waking, drowned me in your eyes.

EL ALBA DENOMINADORA

A embestidas suaves y rosas, la madrugada te iba poniendo nombres:
Sueño equivocado, Ángel sin salida, Mentira de lluvia en bosque.

Al lindero de mi alma que recuerda los ríos,
indecisa, dudó, inmóvil:
¿Vertida estrella, Confusa luz en llanto, Cristal sin voces?

No.
Error de nieve en agua, tu nombre.

THE NAMING DAWN

In onslaughts soft and flushed, the first light was naming you:
Misguided Dream, Angel with No Escape, Lie of Forest Rain.

At the edge of my soul, soul that remembers the rivers,
indecisive, motionless, he hesitated:
Spilled Star, Confused Light in Tears, Crystal Without Voices?

No.
Fallacy of Snow in Water, your name.

EL MAL MINUTO

Cuando para mí eran los trigos viviendas de astros y de dioses
y la escarcha los lloros helados de una gacela,
alguien me enyesó el pecho y la sombra,
traicionándome.

Ese minuto fue el de las balas perdidas,
el del secuestro, por el mar, de los hombres que quisieron ser pájaros,
el del telegrama a deshora y el hallazgo de sangre,
el de la muerte del agua que siempre miró al cielo.

THE VILE MINUTE

When for me the wheat fields were the homes of stars and gods
and frost the frozen cries of a gazelle,
someone encased me, chest and shadow,
betraying me.

That was the minute of stray bullets,
that of kidnapping, by the sea, of the men who wanted to be birds,
that of untimely telegrams and the discovery of blood,
that of water's death, water that always looked up at the sky.

EL ÁNGEL DE LAS BODEGAS

1

Fue cuando la flor del vino se moría en penumbra
y dijeron que el mar la salvaría del sueño.
Aquel día bajé a tientas a tu alma encalada y húmeda.
Y comprobé que un alma oculta frío y escaleras
y que más de una ventana puede abrir con su eco otra voz, si es buena.

Te vi flotar a ti, flor de agonía, flotar sobre tu mismo espíritu.
(Alguien había jurado que el mar te salvaría del sueño.)
Fue cuando comprobé que murallas se quiebran con suspiros
y que hay puertas al mar que se abren con palabras.

2

La flor del vino, muerta en los toneles,
sin haber visto nunca la mar, la nieve.

La flor del vino, sin probar el té,
sin haber visto nunca un piano de cola.

Cuatro arrumbadores encalan los barriles.
Los vinos dulces, llorando, se embarcan a deshora.

La flor del vino blanco, sin haber visto el mar, muerta.
Las penumbras se beben el aceite y un ángel la cera.

THE ANGEL OF THE CELLARS

1

It was when the wine flower was dying in the dark
and they said that the sea would save it from the dream.
That day I felt my way down to your dank and whitewashed soul.
And I confirmed a cold, hidden soul, and stairs,
and that more than one window can open another voice echoing, if it's good.

I saw you floating, flower of agony, floating over your own spirit.
(Someone had sworn that the sea would save you from the dream.)
It was when I verified that walls break with sighs
and that there exist doors to the sea that open with words.

2

Wine flower, dead in your barrels,
without ever having seen the sea, the snow.

Wine flower, without trying the tea,
without ever having seen a grand piano.

Four stock boys whitewashed the barrels.
Sweet wines, weeping, embark at a bad hour.

White wine flower, without having seen the sea, now dead.
The shadows drink the oil and an angel the wax.

He aquí paso a paso toda mi larga historia.
Guardadme el secreto, aceitunas, abejas.

Here, step by step, is my whole long story.
Keep my secret, olives. Keep my secret, bees.

MUERTE Y JUICIO

1

(MUERTE)

A un niño, a un solo niño que iba para piedra nocturna,
para ángel indiferente de una escala sin cielo . . .
Mirad. Conteneos la sangre, los ojos.
A sus pies, él mismo, sin vida.
No aliento de farol moribundo
ni jadeada amarillez de noche agonizante,
sino dos fósforos fijos de pesadilla eléctrica,
clavados sobre su tierra en polvo, juzgándola.
Él resplandor sin salida, lividez sin escape, yacente, juzgándose.

2

(JUICIO)

Tizo electrocutado, infancia mía de ceniza, a mis pies, tizo yacente.
Carbunclo hueco, negro, desprendido de un ángel que iba para piedra
    nocturna,
para límite entre la muerte y la nada.
Tú: yo: niño.

Bambolea el viento un vientre de gritos anteriores al mundo,
a la sorpresa de la luz en los ojos de los recién nacidos,
al descenso de la vía láctea a las gargantas terrestres.
Niño.

Una cuna de llamas, de norte a sur,

DEATH AND JUDGMENT

1
(DEATH)

To a child, to a solitary child who would be a nocturnal stone,
to be an indifferent angel on a ladder with no heaven . . .
Look. Hold back your blood, your eyes.
At his feet, himself, lifeless.
Not the breath of a dying lantern
nor the hard-breathing yellow of an agonizing night,
but two steady fires, matchsticks lit, of an electric nightmare,
nailed to its dusty earth, judging it.
He, blaze with no exit, pallor with no escape, sprawled, judging himself.

2
(JUDGMENT)

Electrocuted chalk, my childhood of ashes, at my feet, tossed chalk.
Hollow, black carbuncle, shaken from an angel who would be a nocturnal
    stone,
to the border between death and nothingness.
You: Me: Child.

The wind rattles the womb of cries prior to the world,
prior to the surprise of light in the eyes of newborns,
the descent of the Milky Way down terrestrial throats.
Child.

A cradle of flames, from north to south,

de frialdad de tiza amortajada en los yelos
a fiebre de paloma agonizando en el área de una bujía,
una cuna de llamas, meciéndote las sonrisas, los llantos.
Niño.

Las primeras palabras, abiertas en las penumbras de los sueños sin nadie
en el silencio rizado de las albercas o en el eco de los jardines,
devoradas por el mar y ocultas hoy en un hoyo sin viento.
Muertas, como el estreno de tus pies en el cansancio frío de una escalera.
Niño.

Las flores, sin piernas para huir de los aires crueles,
de su espoleo continuo al corazón volante de las nieves y los pájaros,
desangradas en un aburrimiento de cartillas y pizarrines.
4 y 4 son 18. Y la X, una K, una H, una J.
Niño.

En un trastorno de ciudades marítimas sin crepúsculos,
de mapas confundidos y desiertos barajados,
atended a unos ojos que preguntan por los afluentes del cielo,
a una memoria extraviada entre nombres y fechas.
Niño.

Perdido entre ecuaciones, triángulos, formulas y precipitados azules,
entre el succso de la sangre, los escombros y las coronas caídas,
cuando los cazadores de oro y el asalto a la banca,
en el rubor tardío de las azoteas
voces de ángeles te anunciaron la botadura y pérdida de tu alma.
Niño.

Y como descendiste al fondo de las mareas,
a las urnas donde el azogue, el plomo y el hierro pretenden ser humanos,

from the coldness of chalk shrouded in the ice
to the fever of a dove agonizing near a candle,
a cradle of flames, rocking your smiles, rocking your tears.
Child.

The first words, open in the shadows of deserted dreams
in the rippling silence of pools or in the echo of gardens,
devoured by the sea and hidden today in a hole without wind.
Dead, like your feet's premiere in the cold fatigue of a staircase.
Child.

The flowers, without legs to flee the cruel winds,
from their continuous spur to the flying heart of snow and birds,
bled dry in the boredom of primers and blackboards.
4 and 4 are 18. And the X, a K, an H, a J.
Child.

In the madness of maritime cities of no sunsets,
of confused maps and shuffled deserts,
pay attention to eyes that ask about the sky's tributaries,
to a memory lost between names and dates.
Child.

Lost among equations, triangles, formulas and blue precipitates,
between bloody events, rubble, and fallen crowns,
when the gold hunters and bank robbery,
in the late blush of rooftops,
voices of angels announced the launch and loss of your soul.
Child.

And as you descended to the bottom of the tides,
to the urns where quicksilver, lead and iron pretend to be human,

tener honores de vida,
a la deriva de la noche tu traje fue dejándote solo.
Niño.

Desnudo, sin los billetes de inocendia fugados en sus bolsillos,
derribada en tu corazón y sola su primera silla,
no creíste ni en Venus que nacía en el compás abierto de tus brazos,
ni en la escala de plumas que tiende el sueño de Jacob al de Julio Verne.
Niño.

Para ir al infierno ho hace falta cambiar de sitio ni postura.

to have life's honors,
drifting through the night, your suit, leaving you behind.
Child.

Naked, without the fugitive tickets of innocence in their pockets,
staggered in your heart and their first chair abandoned,
you believed neither in Venus, who was born in the open compass of your arms,
nor in the staircase of feathers that stretch Jacob's dream into that of Jules Verne.
Child.

To go to Hell it is not necessary to change places or posture.

EXPEDICIÓN

Porque resbalaron hacia el frío los ángeles y las casas,
el ánade y el abeto durmieron nostálgicos aquella noche.
Se sabía que el humo viajaba sin fuego,
que por cada tres osos la luna había perdido seis guardabosques.

Desde lejos, desde muy lejos,
mi alma desempañaba los cristales del tranvía
para hundirse en la niebla movible de los faroles.
La guitarra en la nieve sepultaba a una rosa.
La herradura a una hoja seca.
Un sereno es un desierto.

Se ignora el paradero de la Virgen y las ocas,
la guardida de la escarcha y la habitación de los vientos.
No se sabe si el sur emigró al norte o al oeste,
10,000 dólares de oro a quien se case con la nieve.

Pero he aquí a Eva Gúndersen.

EXPEDITION

Because the angels and the houses slipped into the cold,
the duck and the fir tree slept nostalgic that night.
It was known that smoke travelled without fire,
that for every three bears the moon had lost six rangers.

From far away, from very far away,
my soul will defog the windows of the streetcar
to sink into the moving mist of lanterns.
The guitar in the snow buried a rose.
The horseshoe, a dry leaf.
A watchman is a desert.

Unknown are the whereabouts of the Virgin and the geese,
the den of the frost and the lodgings of the winds.
Unknown whether the south emigrated north or west,
10,000 dollars in gold to whoever marries the snow.

But here is Eva Gundersen.

LOS ÁNGELES COLEGIALES

Ninguno comprendíamos el secreto nocturno de las pizarras,
ni por qué la esfera armilar se exaltaba tan sola cuando la mirábamos.
Sólo sabíamos que una circunferencia puede no ser redonda
y que un eclipse de luna equivoca a las flores
y adelanta el reloj de los pájaros.

Ninguno comprendíamos nada:
ni por qué nuestros dedos eran de tinta china
y la tarde cerraba compases para al alba abrir libros.
Sólo sabíamos que una recta, si quiere, puede ser curva o quebrada
y que las estrellas errantes son niños que ignoran la aritmética.

SCHOOLBOY ANGELS

None of us understood the nocturnal secrets of the blackboards,
or why the armillary sphere glowed only when we looked at it.
We only knew that a circle may not be round
and that a lunar eclipse confuses flowers
and advances the clock of the birds.

None of us understood anything:
not why our fingers were made of Chinese ink
nor why the evening closed compasses to open books at dawn.
We only knew that a straight line, if it wishes, can be curved or broken
and that the wandering stars are children who ignore arithmetic.

NOVELA

En la noche de aquella luna 24,
llovieron en mi cama hojas de cielos marchitos.
A mi alma desprevenida le robaron las palabras.
Su cuerpo fue enterrado a sus pies en un libro.
Era la orden de un monarca.

En el alba de aquella luna 24,
la justicia del frío le cedió el aire de un árbol.
A su sombra, los trineos perdidos
adivinaban rastros de suspiros,
de lloros extraviados.
En su sombra se oía el silencio de los castillos.

En el día de aquella luna 24,
fue ajusticiada mi alma por la niebla
que un suicida lento de noviembre
había olvidado en mi estancia.
Era la última voluntad de un monarca.

A ROMANCE

On the night of that twenty-fourth moon,
leaves from desiccated skies rained onto my bed.
My unsuspecting soul was robbed of words.
Its body was buried in a book at its feet.
It was the order of a monarch.

In the dawn of that twenty-fourth moon,
the justice of the cold gave up the air of a tree.
In its shadow, the lost sleighs
divined traces of sighs,
of stray tears.
In its shadow, one could hear the silence of castles.

On the day of the twenty-fourth moon,
my soul was put to death by the mist
that a slow suicide in November
had forgotten during my stay.
It was the last wish of a monarch.

NIEVE VIVA

Sin mentir, ¡qué mentira de nieve anduvo muda por mi sueño!
Nieve sin voz, quizás de ojos azules, lenta y con cabellos.
¿Cuándo la nieve al mirar distraída movió bucles de fuego?
Anduvo muda blanqueando las preguntas que no se respondieron,
los olvidados y borrados sepulcros para estrenar nuevos recuerdos.
Dando a cenizas, ya en el aire, forma de luz sin hueso.

LIVING SNOW

Without lying, tell me what lie of snow walked mute through my dream!
Voiceless snow, with blue eyes perhaps, slow and with hair.
When did the snow, looking distracted, push coils of fire?
It walked mute, whitewashing the unanswered questions,
the forgotten and crossed out sepulchers, to launch new memories.
Giving to ashes, already airborne, the shape of boneless light.

INVITACIÓN AL ARPA

1

Lejos, lejos.
Adonde las estancias olvidan guantes de polvo
y las consolas sueñan párpados y nombres ya idos.
Un sombrero se hastía
y unos lazos sin bucles se cansan.
Si las violetas se aburren,
es porque están nostálgicas de moaré y abanicos.

Lejos, más lejos.
A los cielos rasos donde las goteras
abren sus mapas húmedos para que viajen los lechos.
Adonde los muelles se hunden sin esperanza
y rostros invisibles avetan los espejos.
Al país de las telas de araña.

2

Más lejos, mucho más lejos.
A la luna disecada entre la hoja de un álamo y la passion de un libro.
Sé que hay yelos nocturnos que ocultan candelabros
y que la muerte tiembla en el sueño movible de las bujías.
Un maniquí de luto agoniza sobre un nardo.
Una voz desde el olvido mueve el agua dormida de los pianos.
Siempre, siempre más lejos.
Adonde las maderas guardan ecos y sombras de pasos,
adonde las polillas desvelan el silencio de las corbatas,
adonde todo un siglo es un arpa en abandono.

INVITATION TO THE HARP

1

Far, far away.
Where the rooms forget dust gloves
And consoles dream of eyelids and names already gone.
A hat grows weary of itself
and loopless ribbons fatigue.
If the violets get bored,
it is due to their nostalgia for moiré and fans.

Far, farther away.
To the bare skies where the raindrops
open their wet maps for the beds to travel.
Where the docks sink hopeless,
and invisible faces vein the mirrors.
To the land of spiderwebs.

2

Farther away, much farther away.
To the moon stuffed between the leaf of a poplar and the passion of a book.
I know there exist nocturnal frosts that obscure candelabras
and that death trembles in the moveable dreams of the candles.
A mourning mannequin agonizes over a spikenard.
A voice from oblivion stirs the sleeping water of the pianos.
Always, always farther away.
Where the wood planks keep echoes and shadows of footsteps,
where moths reveal the silence of neckties,
where an entire century is an abandoned harp.

LUNA ENEMIGA

Como al chocar los astros contra mi pecho no veía,
fui hundiéndome de espaldas en los cielos pasados.
Diez reyes del otoño contra mí se rebelaron.
Ángeles y traiciones siempre aceleran las caídas.
Una hoja, un hombre.
En tu órbita se quemaba mi sangre, luna enemiga.

Salvadme de los años en estado de nebulosa,
de los espejos que pronuncian trajes y páginas desvanecidos,
de las manos estampadas en los recuerdos que bostezan.
Huid.
Nos entierran en viento enemigo.

Y es que mi alma ha olvidado las reglas.

ENEMY MOON

As I could not see the stars colliding against my chest,
I was sinking backwards into past skies.
Ten kings of autumn rebelled against me.
Angels and betrayals always accelerate falls.
A leaf, a man.
In your orbit my blood burned, enemy moon.

Save me from years in a state of nebula,
from the mirrors that pronounced faded suits and pages,
from the hands stamped in yawning memories.
Save yourself.
They bury us in enemy wind.

And so it is, my soul has forgotten the rules.

CASTIGOS

Es cuando golfos y bahías de sangre,
coagulados de astros difuntos y vengativos,
inundan los sueños.
Cuando golfos y bahías de sangre
atropellan la navegación de los lechos
y a la diestra del mundo muere olvidado un ángel.
Cuando saben a azufre los vientos
y las bocas nocturnas a hueso, vidrio y alambre.
Oídme.

Yo no sabía que las puertas cambiaban de sitio,
que las almas podían ruborizarse de sus cuerpos,
ni que al final de un túnel la luz traía la muerte.
Oídme aún.

Quieren huir los que duermen.
Pero esas tumbas del mar no son fijas,
esas tumbas que se abren por abandono y cansancio del cielo no son es-
tables,
y las albas tropiezan con rostros desfigurados.
Oídme aún. Más todavía.

Hay noches en que las horas se hacen de piedra en los espacios,
en que las venas no andan
y los silencios yerguen siglos y dioses futuros.
Un relámpago baraja las lenguas y trastorna las palabras.
Pensad en las esfereas derruidas,
en las órbitas secas de los hombres deshabitados,

PUNISHMENTS

It's when gulfs and bays of blood,
coagulated with dead and vengeful stars,
inundate the dreams.
When gulfs and bays of blood
trample the navigation of facts
and at the right hand of the world an angel dies forgotten.
When the winds taste of sulfur,
and the nocturnal mouths of bone, glass, and wire.
Hear me.

I did not know that doors change places,
that souls could blush from their bodies,
or that the end of a tunnel light brought death.
Hear me still.

Those who sleep want to escape.
But those tombs of the sea are not fixed,
those tombs that open by way of abandon and fatigue of the sky are not
stable,
and daybreaks stumble upon disfigured faces.
Hear me still. There is more still.

There are nights when, in space, the hours turn to stone,
in which the veins do not walk
and the silences erect centuries and future gods.
Lightning shuffles the tongues and scrambles the words.
Think of the ruined spheres,
of the dry orbits of uninhabited men,

en los milenios mudos.
Más, más todavía. Oídme.

Se ve que los cuerpos no están en donde estaban,
que la luna se enfría de ser mirada
y que el llanto de un niño deforma las constelaciones.
Cielos enmohecidos nos oxidan las frentes desiertas,
donde cada minuto sepulta su cadáver sin nombre.
Oídme, oídme por ultimo.

Porque siempre hay un ultimo posterior a la caída de los páramos,
al advenimiento del frío en los sueños que se descuidan,
a los derrumbos de la muerte sobre el esqueleto de la nada.

of the silent millennia.
There is more, more still. Hear me.

One can see that the bodies are not where they were,
that the moon grows cold from scrutiny
and that a child's cry deforms the constellations.
Moldy skies rust our deserted brows,
where each minute buries a corpse with no name.
Hear me, hear me finally.

Because there is always one left after the fall of badlands,
the advent of cold in neglected dreams,
the collapse of death on the skeleton of nothingness.

EL ÁNGEL FALSO

Para que yo anduviera entre los nudos de las raíces
y la viviendas óseas de los gusanos.
Para que yo escuchara los crujidos descompuestos del mundo
y mordiera la luz petrificada de los astros,
al oeste de mi sueño levantaste tu tienda, ángel falso.

Los que unidos por una misma corriente de agua me veis,
los que atados por una traición y la caída de una estrella m escucháis,
acogeos a las voces abandonadas de las ruinas.
Oíd la lentitud de una piedra que se dobla hacia la muerte.

No os soltéis de las manos.

Hay arañas que agonizan sin nido
y yedras que al contacto de un hombro se incendian y llueven sangre.
La luna transparenta el esqueleto de los lagartos.
Si os acordáis del cielo,
la cólera del frío se erguirá aguda een los cardos
o en el disimulo de las zanjas que estrangulan
el único descanso de las auroras: las aves.
Quienes piensen en los vivos verán moldes de arcilla
habitados por ángeles inficles, infatigables:
los ángeles sonámbulos que gradúan las órbitas de la fatiga.

¿Para qué seguir andando?
Las humedades son íntimas de los vidrios en punta
y después de un mal sueño la escarcha despierta clavos
o tijeras capaces de helar el luto de los cuervos.

THE FALSE ANGEL

So that I might walk among the knots of roots
and the bone house of the worms.
So that I might listen to the broken rustlings of the world
and bite the petrified light of the stars,
to the west of my dream you pitched your tent, false angel.

Those of you who, united by the same stream of water, see me,
those who, bound by betrayal, and the fall of a star, listen to me,
take refuge in the abandoned voices of the ruins.
Hear the slowness of a stone that bends toward death.

Don't let go of your hands.

There are spiders dying without nests
and ivy that, at the touch of a shoulder, catches and rains blood.
The moon makes transparent the skeletons of lizards.
If you remember the sky,
the anger of the cold will rise sharp in the thistles
or in the duplicity of ditches that strangle
the only repose of daybreak: the birds.
Those who consider the living will see molds of clay
inhabited by faithless, indefatigable angels:
sleepwalking angels that calibrate the orbits of fatigue.

Why keep walking?
Humidity clings to the pointed glass
and after a bad dream the frost awakens nails
and scissors capable of freezing the crows in mourning.

Todo ha terminado.

Puedes envanecerte, en la cauda marchita de los cometas que se hunden,

de que mataste a un muerto,

de que diste a una sombra la longitud desvelada del llanto,

de que asfixiarte el estertor de las capas atmosféricas.

Everything is done.
You can boast, amid the withered tails of sinking comets,
that you murdered one of the dead,
that you gave a shadow the sleepless length of tears,
that you choked the death rattle from the atmospheric strata.

LOS ÁNGELES DE LAS RUINAS

Pero por fin llegó el día, la hora de las palas y los cubos.
No esperaba la luz que se vinieran abajo los minutos
porque distraía en el mar la nostalgia terrestre de los ahogados.
Nadie esperaba que los cielos amanecieran de esparto
ni que los ángeles ahuyentaran sobre los hombres astros de cardenillo.

Los trajes no esperaban tan pronto la emigración de los cuerpos.
Por un alba navegable huía la aridez de los lechos.

Se habla de la bencina,
de las catástrofes que causan los olvidos inexplicables.
Se murmura en el cielo de la traición de la rosa.
Yo comento con mi alma el contrabando de la pólvora,
a la izquierda del cadáver de un ruiseñor amigo mío.
No os acerquéis.

Nunca pensasteis que vuestra sombra volvería a la sombra
cuando una bala de revólver hiriera mi silencio.
Pero al fin llegó ese segundo,
disfrazado de noche que espera un epitafio.
La cal viva es el fondo que mueve la proyección de los muertos.

Os he dicho que no os acerquéis.
Os he pedido un poco de distancia:
la mínima para comprender un sueño
y un hastío sin rumbo haga estallar las flores y las calderas.

La luna era muy tierna antes de los atropellos
y solía descender a los hornos por las chimeneas de las fábricas.

THE ANGELS OF RUINS

But the day finally came, the hour of shovels and buckets.
I did not expect the light to collapse the minutes
because I was distracted by the terrestrial nostalgia of those drowned at sea.
No one expected the heavens to wake from esparto grass
nor that angels would chase men away with verdigris stars.

Suits did not expect the emigration of bodies so soon.
Through a navigable dawn escaped the barrenness of beds.

There is talk of gasoline,
of the catastrophes that cause inexplicable forgetfulness.
There are whispers, in heaven, of the betrayal of the rose.
I complain to my soul about the smuggling of gunpowder,
to the left of the corpse of my friend the nightingale.
Don't come near.

You never thought that your shadow would return to shadow
when a revolver's bullet bore through my silence.
But in the end that second arrived,
disguised as night awaiting an epitaph.
Quicklime is the base that broadcasts the dead.

I told you not to come near.
I have asked you for a little distance:
the minimum required to comprehend a dream
and an aimless weariness to make flowers and cauldrons explode.

The moon was very tender before the abuses
and used to descend into furnaces through the chimneys of factories.

Ahora fallece impure en un mapa imprevisto de petróleo,
asistida por un ángel que le acelera la agonía.
Hombres de cinc, alquitrán y plomo la olvidan.

Se olvidan hombres de brea y fango
que sus buques y sus trenes,
a vista de pájaro,
son ya en medio del mundo una mancha de aceite,
limitada de cruces por todas partes.
Se han olvidado.

Como yo, como todos.
Y nadie espera ya la llegada del expreso,
la visita oficial de la luz a los mares necesitados,
la resurrección de las voces en los ecos que se calcinan.

Now she's dying impure on an unforeseen map of gasoline,
assisted by an angel who accelerates her agony.
Men of zinc, tar, and lead forget her.

Men of tar and mud forget
that their ships and their trains,
from a bird's-eye view,
are already a stain of oil in the middle of the world,
bound by crosses on all sides.
They have forgotten.

Like me, like everyone.
And no one waits, now, for the arrival of the express,
the official visit of light to seas in need,
the resurrection of voices in smoldering echoes.

LOS ÁNGELES MUERTOS

Buscad, buscadlos:
en el insomnio de las cañerias olvidadas,
en los cauces interrumpidos por el silencio de las basuras.
No lejos de los charcos incapaces de guardar una nube,
unos ojos perdidos,
una sortija rota
o una estrella pisoteada.

Porque yo los he visto:
en esos escombros momentáneos que aparecen en las neblinas.
Porque yo los he tocado:
en el destierro de un ladrillo difunto,
venido a la nada desde una torre o un carro.
Nunca más allá de las chimeneas que se derrumban
ni de esas hojas tenaces que se estampan en los zapatos.
En todo esto.
Mas en esas astillas vagabundas que se consumen sin fuego,
en esas ausencias hundidas que sufren los muebles desvencijados,
no a mucha distancia de los nombres y signos que se enfrían en las paredes.

Buscad, buscadlos:
debajo de la gota de cera que sepulta la palabra de un libro
o la firma de uno de esos rincones de cartas
que trae rodando el polvo.
Cerca del casco perdido de una botella,
de una suela extraviada en la nieve,
de una navaja de afeitar abandonada al borde de un precipicio.

THE DEAD ANGELS

Search, search for them:
In the insomnia of forgotten drains,
in the sewers interrupted by the silence of sewage.
Not far from the puddles unable to keep a cloud,
lost eyes,
a broken ring,
or a trampled star.

Because I have seen them:
In that momentary debris that appears in the mist.
Because I have touched them:
In the banishment of an out-of-work brick,
come to nothing from a tower or a car.
Never beyond the collapsing chimneys
or those tenacious leaves that press themselves to shoes.
In all of this.
Even in those vagabond splinters consumed with no fire,
in those sunken absences suffered by rickety fittings,
not far from the names and signs cooling on the walls.

Search, search for them:
Under the wax drop that buries the book's word
or the signature from one of these corners of letters
that brings, swirling, the dust.
Near the lost helmet of a bottle,
a shoe sole lost in the snow,
a razor abandoned at the edge of a cliff.

LOS ÁNGELES FEOS

Vosotros habéis sido,
vosotros que dormís en el vaho sin suerte de los pantanos
para que el alba más desgraciada os reanime en una gloria de estiércol,
vosotros habéis sido la causa de este viaje.

Ni un solo pájaro es capaz de beber en un alma
cuando sin haberlo querido un cielo se entrecruza con otro
y una piedra cualquiera levanta a un astro una calumnia.

Ved.

La luna cae mordida por el ácido nítrico
en las charcas donde el amoníaco aprieta la codicia de los alacranes.
Si os atravéis a dar un paso,
sabrán los siglos venideros que la bondad de las aguas es aparente
cuantas más hoyas y lodos ocultan los paisajes.
La lluvia me persigue atirantando cordeles.
Será lo más seguro que hombre se convierta en estopa.

Mirad esto:
ha sido un falso testimonio decir que una soga al cuello no es agradable
y que el excremento de la golondrina exalta al mes de mayo.
Pero yo os digo:
una rosa es más rosa habitada por las orugas
que sobre la nieve marchita de esta luna de quince años.

Mirad esto también, antes que demos sepultura al viaje:
cuando una sombra se entrecoge las uñas en las bisagras de las puertas

THE UGLY ANGELS

You have been,
you who sleep in the luckless vapor of swamps
so that the most unfortunate dawn may revive you in a glory of dung,
you have been the cause of this journey.

Not a single bird is capable of drinking from a soul
when, without wanting to, one sky intersects with another
and any ordinary stone can raise slander against a star.

Look.

The moon falls, bitten by nitric acid,
into the puddles where ammonia strangles the greed of scorpions.
If you dare take a step,
the centuries to come will know the goodness of the waters is apparent
the more holes and mud the landscapes hide.
The rain pursues me, tightening cords.
Safest to say, a man will be converted to burlap.

Look at this:
It was perjury to say that a noose around the neck is not pleasant
and that the songbird's excrement exalts the month of May.
But I say to you:
a rose is more rose when inhabited by caterpillars
than on the withered snow of this fifteen-year-old moon.

Look at this too, before we bury the journey:
when a shadow catches its fingernails in the door hinges

o el pie helado de un ángel sufre el insomnio fijo de una piedra,
mi alma sin saberlo se perfecciona.

Al fin ya vamos a hundirnos.
Es hora de que me dierais la mano
y me arañarais la poca luz que coge un agujero al cerrarse
y me matarais esta mala palabra que voy a pinchar sobre las tierras que se derriten.

or an angel's frozen foot suffers the fixed insomnia of a stone,
my soul, without knowing it, perfects itself.

In the end, we will ruin ourselves.
It is time you gave me your hand
and scratched into me the little light that catches a hole as it closes
and killed for me this evil word I plan to plunge into the thawing earth.

EL ÁNGEL SUPERVIVIENTE

Acordaos.

La nieve traía gotas de lacre, de plomo derretido

y disimulos de niña que ha dado muerte a un cisne.

Una mano enguantada, la dispersión de la luz y el lento asesinato.

La derrota del cielo, un amigo.

Acordaos de aquel día, acordaos

y no olvidéis que la sorpresa paralizó el pulso y el color de los astros.

En el frío, muurieron dos fantasmas.

Por un ave, tres anillos de oro

fueron hallados y enterrados en la escarcha.

La última voz de un hombre ensangrentó el viento.

Todos los ángeles perdieron la vida.

Menos uno, herido, alicortado.

THE SURVIVING ANGEL

Remember.
The snow brought drops of sealing wax, molten lead
and the cunning of a girl who killed a swan.
A gloved hand, the scattering of light and a slow murder.
The sky's defeat, a friend's.

Remember that day, remember
and don't forget that the surprise paralyzed the pulse and the color of stars.
In the cold, two phantoms died.
By a bird, three gold rings
were found and buried in the frost.
The last voice of a man bloodied the wind.
All the angels lost their lives.
Except one, wounded, its wings clipped.

ACKNOWLEDGMENTS

Mil gracias to the editors of the following publications in which some of these translations first appeared: Elizabeth Scanlon at *American Poetry Review*, John Hennessy at *The Common*, Dora Malek at *The Hopkins Review*, Adam Ross at *The Sewanee Review*, and Meghan O'Rourke at *The Yale Review*.

Gracias to friends and family who encouraged and supported this work along the way, particularly: Ama Codjoe, Robert Pinsky, Patrick Rosal, Clarisse Baleja Saidi, Nicole Sealey, David St. John, and Jorrell Watkins.

Gracias to the following institutions for time, space, and other invaluable resources that made this work possible: The Fine Arts Work Center in Provincetown, Hermitage Foundation, the University of Arizona Poetry Center, and Wesleyan University.

Gracias to Fred "Perm Dude" Courtright for securing North American translation rights.

Gracias to Carles Masdeu of Angencia Literaria Carmen Balcells, S.A., for granting said rights.

Gracias to Tim's Used Books in Provincetown, MA, for selling me that gigantic, old, waterlogged Spanish-English dictionary for two dollars. Best money I've ever spent.

Gracias to Anya, Anna, and the crew at Blue Flower Arts for EVERYTHING you do!

Gracias to Martha, Ryan, Sally, Bridget, and the rest of the family at Four Way Books for believing in this project and for making it happen.

Gracias and a surreptitious head nod to my well-dwellers and Tres Leches gente.

Finalmente, gracias y gracias y more insufficient and unspeakable gracias to and for and onto and because of one, Nicole Sealey. Didn't think it appropriate to include a dedication page for someone else's poems, but *if you don't knoooow, now you know*. This book is for you.

ABOUT THE AUTHORS

Considered one of the major Spanish poets of the 20th century, Rafael Alberti (1902–1999) was the author of over twenty volumes of poetry, including *Marinero en Tierra, Cal y Canto,* and *La Amante.* He also wrote several plays and the celebrated memoir, *La Arboleda Perdida (The Lost Grove).* His many honors include the Premio Cervantes, the America Award, and the Lenin Peace Prize among others. *Sobre Los ángeles (Concerning the Angels)* is regarded by many as his magnum opus.

John Murillo is the author of the poetry collections *Up Jump the Boogie* and *Kontemporary Amerikan Poetry.* His honors include the Kingsley Tufts Poetry Award, the Four Quartets Prize from the T.S. Eliot Foundation and the Poetry Society of America, and the Lucille Clifton Legacy Award from St. Mary's College of Maryland. He is a professor of English and teaches in the MFA program at Hunter College.

PUBLICATION OF THIS BOOK WAS MADE POSSIBLE
BY GRANTS AND DONATIONS. WE ARE ALSO GRATEFUL
TO THOSE INDIVIDUALS WHO PARTICIPATED IN
OUR BUILD A BOOK PROGRAM. THEY ARE:

Anonymous (14), Robert Abrams, Debra Allbery, Nancy Allen, Michael
Ansara, Kathy Aponick, Jean Ball, Sally Ball, Jill Bialosky, Sophie Cabot
Black, Laurel Blossom, Tommye Blount, Karen and David Blumenthal,
Jonathan Blunk, Lee Briccetti, Jane Martha Brox, Mary Lou Buschi,
Anthony Cappo, Carla and Steven Carlson, Robin Rosen Chang, Liza
Charlesworth, Peter Coyote, Elinor Cramer, Kwame Dawes, Michael Anna
de Armas, Brian Komei Dempster, Renko and Stuart Dempster, Matthew
DeNichilo, Rosalynde Vas Dias, Patrick Donnelly, Charles R. Douthat,
Lynn Emanuel, Blas Falconer, Laura Fjeld, Carolyn Forché, Helen Fremont
and Donna Thagard, Debra Gitterman, Dorothy Tapper Goldman, Alison
Granucci, Elizabeth T. Gray Jr., Naomi Guttman and Jonathan Meade,
Jeffrey Harrison, KT Herr, Carlie Hoffman, Melissa Hotchkiss, Thomas and
Autumn Howard, Catherine Hoyser, Elizabeth Jackson, Linda Susan Jackson,
Jessica Jacobs, Deborah Jonas-Walsh, Jennifer Just, Voki Kalfayan, Maeve
Kinkead, Victoria Korth, David Lee and Jamila Trindle, Rodney Terich
Leonard, Howard Levy, Owen Lewis and Susan Ennis, Eve Linn, Matthew
Lippman, Ralph and Mary Ann Lowen, Maja Lukic, Neal Lulofs, Anthony
Lyons, Ricardo Alberto Maldonado, Trish Marshall, Donna Masini, Deborah
McAlister, Carol Moldaw, Michael and Nancy Murphy, Kimberly Nunes,
Matthew Olzmann and Vievee Francis, Veronica Patterson, Patrick Phillips,
Robert Pinsky, Megan Pinto, Kevin Prufer, Anna Duke Reach, Paula Rhodes,
Yoana Setzer, James Shalek, Soraya Shalforoosh, Peggy Shinner,   Joan
Silber, Jane Simon, Debra Spark, Donna Spruijt-Metz, Arlene Stang, Page
Hill Starzinger, Catherine Stearns, Yerra Sugarman, Arthur Sze, Laurence
Tancredi, Marjorie and Lew Tesser, Peter Turchi, Connie Voisine, Susan
Walton, Martha Webster and Robert Fuentes, Calvin Wei, Allison Benis
White, Lauren Yaffe, and Rolf Yngve.